HIP-HOP
Biographies

LIL
WAYNE

SADDLEBACK
PUBLISHING

HIP-HOP Biographies

Chris Brown
Drake
50 Cent
Jay-Z
Nicki Minaj

Pitbull
Rihanna
Usher
Lil Wayne
Kanye West

SADDLEBACK
PUBLISHING
www.sdlback.com

ISBN-13: 978-1-62250-014-7
ISBN-10: 1-62250-014-8
eBook: 978-1-61247-695-7

Printed in Guangzhou, China
NOR/1112/CA21201417
17 16 15 14 13   1 2 3 4 5

Table of Contents

Timeline

1982: Dwayne Michael Carter Jr. is born in New Orleans, Louisiana.

1994: Lil Wayne signs a recording contract with Cash Money Records.

1995: Wayne accidentally shoots himself.

1997: Lil Wayne joins the hip-hop group The Hot Boys.

The Hot Boys release the album *Get It How U Live!*

1998: Lil Wayne's daughter Reginae is born.

1999: Lil Wayne releases *Tha Block Is Hot.*

2000: Wayne releases his second album, *Lights Out.*

2004: Wayne marries his daughter's mother, Toya.

Lil Wayne releases *Tha Carter.*

2005: Hurricane Katrina hits New Orleans.

He releases *Tha Carter II.*

Wayne heads up his own record label, Young Money Records.

2006: Toya and Lil Wayne divorce.

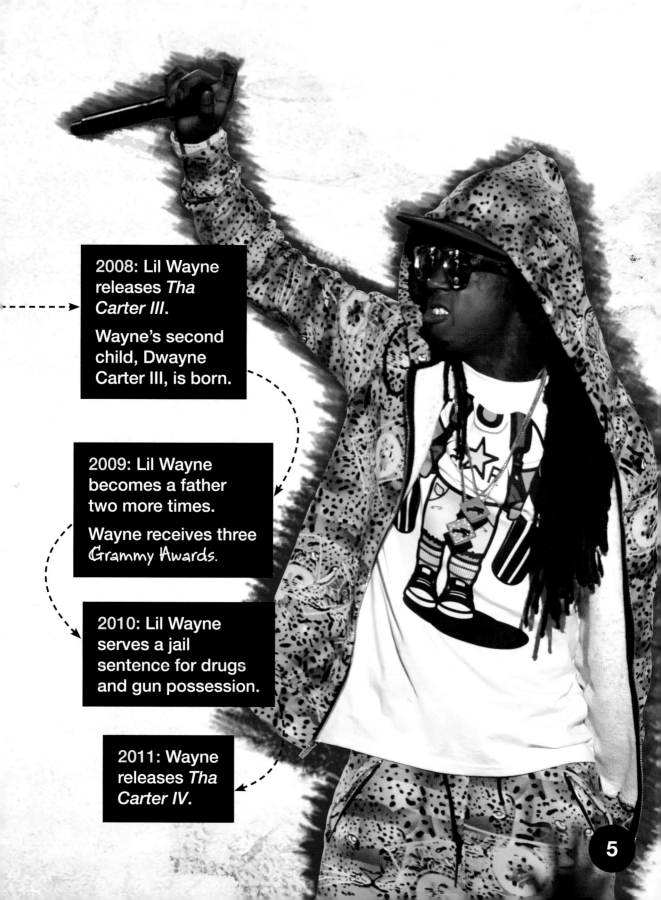

2008: Lil Wayne releases *Tha Carter III*.

Wayne's second child, Dwayne Carter III, is born.

2009: Lil Wayne becomes a father two more times.

Wayne receives three Grammy Awards.

2010: Lil Wayne serves a jail sentence for drugs and gun possession.

2011: Wayne releases *Tha Carter IV*.

Southern Roots

Lil Wayne is one of those artists with a trademark appearance. He wears his hair in dreadlocks. He is rarely seen without a red bandana hanging out of a pocket or tied to his arm or leg. His teeth are covered in gold, platinum, and diamonds. His body is covered with tattoos. But he uses the tattoos to describe his life. He said, "I have 'misunderstood' tattooed on my face because I do feel that a lot of times I'm very misunderstood."

Lil Wayne also has a reputation for being a gangster. In an interview he explained what it means to be a gangster. He said, "I don't take nothin' from no one. I do what I wanna do. And I'm gonna do that until the day I die. And if I can't do that, then I'll just die." This attitude helps show people how confident he is. Lil Wayne bragged, "You can't compare any other artist out there to me. They are them, I am me. Nobody can do what I can. I am the best at what I do and that's everything."

Lil Wayne can have this much swagger because he has so many fans. Through his music he has changed the language of hip-hop. He came up with words like "bling." He taught people to "drop it like it's hot." Superstars like Justin Timberlake love "Weezy's" raspy voice. They also understand that Lil Wayne is not a record company's latest ready-made star. He sets his own rules and does not let people tell him how to make his music.

Lil Wayne is known for his tattoos and the grill on his teeth.

Dwayne Michael Carter Jr. was born on September 27, 1982. He grew up in the Hollygrove neighborhood in New Orleans, Louisiana. The neighborhood was quite poor. Dwayne's mother, Jacinda, was only nineteen when she had Dwayne. She could not afford to care for herself and her son alone. So Jacinda moved in with her boyfriend's mother. Her boyfriend was Lil Wayne's father. But he did not do much to help raise his son.

What Dwayne's father did do was abuse Jacinda. So she moved away from his mother's home. She put Dwayne in school. By the time he was eight years old, he was earning straight As. He would also rap for anyone who would listen. He remembered, "I was the only child, so whenever anybody came to the house, it was showtime. I couldn't wait."

When Dwayne was still in elementary school, his mother met and married Reginald "Rabbit" McDonald. Rabbit became Dwayne's stepfather. He was the only real father Dwayne ever knew. Rabbit moved Jacinda and Dwayne out of Hollygrove to a safer neighborhood. But Rabbit did not lead a safe life. He made money by selling drugs. Just four years after marrying Jacinda, Rabbit was murdered.

Dwayne was still a good student. He attended an elementary school for gifted students. He loved sports too. But music was Dwayne's strongest talent. He even had a rap name. Dwayne called himself Gangsta D.

Dwayne later decided to drop his first name. He was named after his father, but his father was not part of his life. Wayne wanted a name that was all his own.

Dwayne grew up in a poor neighborhood in New Orleans, Louisiana.

Wayne's home life was a mess. But his focus on his music would give him hope. Cash Money Records opened in New Orleans. Brothers Bryan "Birdman" and Ronald "Slim" Williams owned it. Most record companies were based in New York or Los Angeles. So a hometown record company was a big deal.

Wayne saw Birdman and Slim in a neighborhood record store. He walked right up to the brothers and started rapping. Birdman and Slim were impressed with him, so they gave him their business card. This was a way of saying, "Call us when you are old enough to work." But to Wayne, all it meant was, "Call us!"

Wayne called the brothers' answering machine every day. He left messages with freestyle raps. Finally the brothers agreed to let him do odd jobs around the Cash Money office. Birdman took Wayne under his wing. They became so close that Wayne started calling him "Pa."

When Wayne was eleven years old, Birdman and Slim offered Wayne a contract. Wayne was a professional rapper in the sixth grade! He believes being from New Orleans gave him the confidence he needed. He said, "We have this motivation. You see people on the corner, singing, and that takes a different type of pride to do that … I think that's why me, being eleven, looking at this man who's intimidating the world, he tells me to rap, and I rap. He didn't ask me to tell him about who I am. I probably would have froze up. But music, rap music—I think that's where New Orleans comes in. We're relentless when it comes to music."

The Williams brothers offered Wayne a record contract when he was eleven years old.

Teen Rapper

Wayne's mother went to high school with Birdman and Slim. She knew they had bad reputations. After Wayne signed his contract, his grades fell. He also started using drugs. Jacinda put her foot down. She said that Wayne could not be around the Williams brothers any more.

Wayne's friend Cortez Bryant helped Wayne get back on track. He encouraged Wayne to bring his grades up. He got Wayne to join the band, where he played the cymbals. Wayne also joined his middle school's drama club. He acted in *The Wizard of Oz*.

Jacinda agreed that Wayne had changed for the better. She allowed Wayne to work with Birdman and Slim again. But Wayne had to agree to her conditions. He had to keep up his grades. He had to stay away from drugs. And he was not allowed to use *profanity* in his raps.

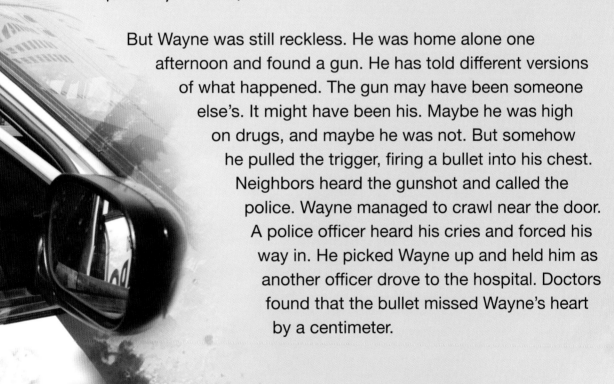

But Wayne was still reckless. He was home alone one afternoon and found a gun. He has told different versions of what happened. The gun may have been someone else's. It might have been his. Maybe he was high on drugs, and maybe he was not. But somehow he pulled the trigger, firing a bullet into his chest. Neighbors heard the gunshot and called the police. Wayne managed to crawl near the door. A police officer heard his cries and forced his way in. He picked Wayne up and held him as another officer drove to the hospital. Doctors found that the bullet missed Wayne's heart by a centimeter.

A New Orleans police officer saved Wayne after he shot himself.

Cash Money Records had a few young rappers under contract. B.G. and Juvenile were already fairly popular around the southern United States. Young Turk and Wayne joined the two better-known rappers to form the group The Hot Boys. Wayne was now using the name Lil Wayne.

Cash Money had a *producer*, Mannie Fresh, work with the four boys. He made sure that each of the rappers had a unique sound. They would take turns rapping, one trying to outdo the next. Mannie collected fifteen songs and set out to make an album. On some tracks, the four rapped together. On others, a rapper might perform solo. Mannie also invited other popular hip-hop artists to perform on some songs.

Wayne was part of the boy band The Hot Boys.

Wayne thought that his music career was more important than school. So in 1996 he dropped out of high school. Not long after quitting school, his high-school girlfriend announced that she was pregnant. Lil Wayne would become a father.

The Hot Boys worked hard recording. They also made appearances around Louisiana and other southern cities. Pop "boy bands" were very popular at the time. Cash Money made The Hot Boys a rap "boy band." The boys wore clothes that teen rap fans in the South started copying. They used slang that kids copied. Finally Cash Money released their album *Get It How U Live* in 1997. The album sold over 400,000 copies. Cash Money could not afford to pay for advertising. The sales were simply because of the group's public appearances. They earned their fans all by themselves.

Selling so many records without a big company to *promote* it was astounding. Cash Money and The Hot Boys caught the attention of major record companies. Cash Money made a deal with Universal Records. Universal would help sell The Hot Boys' music. In 1999 Universal rereleased *Get It How U Live*. Then The Hot Boys released their second album, *Guerrilla Warfare*, a few months later. With Universal's support, the album ranked number one on *Billboard's* Top Hip-Hop album charts.

PARENTAL
ADVISORY
EXPLICIT CONTENT

The **Parental Advisory**
is a notice to parents
that recordings identified
by this logo may contain strong language
or depictions of violence,
sex or substance abuse.
Parental discretion is advised.

Cash Money also had solo albums from B.G., Juvenile, and Lil Wayne the same year. The success of the group pushed the sales of the solo albums. Lil Wayne's 1999 solo album was called *Tha Block Is Hot*. The first single from the album was a song by the same name. The week the album came out, it reached number three on the *Billboard* Top 200 album chart. It sold over one million copies. By the time Lil Wayne was seventeen years old, he was a millionaire.

The Recording Industry Association of America (RIAA) sets rules about how music is made. One of their rules is about minor artists. Minors cannot record lyrics with profanity. Wayne was one of the younger performers in The Hot Boys. If a song used a curse word, an older rapper took those lines. But Lil Wayne was a minor when he recorded *Tha Block Is Hot*. So the album did not have a curse word on it. The record still received the RIAA "parental advisory" sticker. It warned people buying the record that the content may be vulgar to some. Lil Wayne may not have used curse words, but his songs were about sex, drugs, and violence.

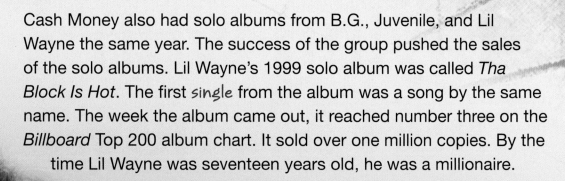

The Recording Industry Association of America made rules that prevented Wayne from cursing on his first records.

Staying with Cash Money

Lil Wayne followed *Tha Block Is Hot* with *Lights Out* in 2000. The album did not sell as well as his first album. But it still reached number sixteen on the *Billboard* Top 200 album chart. Two years

later he released his third album, *500 Degreez*. It reached number six on the same chart. Both records sold more than half a million copies. But this was nowhere near the success of *Tha Block Is Hot*.

The other members of The Hot Boys released albums too. They also recorded songs together. None of them were very successful. Gradually B.G., Young Turk, and Juvenile all left Cash Money Records. The rappers that made the company millions were gone, except for Lil Wayne. Rumors in the record industry were that Cash Money was going out of business.

Lil Wayne had faith in Birdman. He even called himself "Birdman Jr." The two men also knew that they needed to do something different to get Wayne's career back on track. They were planning an album for release in 2003. They gave up on the album in favor of something new. Wayne would release a mixtape in 2004, *Da Drought*.

For years Wayne had written his rhymes. He kept them in a notebook. When he recorded *Da Drought*, he rapped all of the lyrics he had left in the notebook. Listeners can even hear him turn the pages on his songs. When he was through recording, he put the notebook away. He did not write down a song again. All of his songs from that point on came out of his head.

Lil Wayne stayed with Birdman when Cash Money was struggling.

Cash Money and Lil Wayne wanted to get his music onto more radio stations and CD players. The mixtape was not sold like an album would be. Instead, it was sent for free to radio stations and dance clubs. If the DJs liked the mixtape, they would play it. Audiences would hear it and look for it in the stores. But because mixtapes are not for sale, fans would not find the music. But they would get excited, waiting for an album.

The plan worked. Lil Wayne's next album, *Tha Carter*, was released in 2004. The album sold over 800,000 copies. It topped the Hip-Hop Album charts. It was the first record Wayne made without writing his songs first. Critics noticed that his songs were better. Fans loved the single "Go DJ." So did the DJs that the song honored. The song reached number five on the *Billboard* Hot 100 singles chart. That meant it was competing against other types of music, such as pop and R&B.

Lil Wayne worked with Destiny's Child in 2004. He rapped on their song, "Soldier." The single reached number three on the *Billboard* Hot 100 singles chart. Lil Wayne was finally reaching more than just hip-hop fans.

In 2005 Lil Wayne released more mixtapes. It built up excitement over the next album he would release. *Tha Carter II* came out in 2005. The week it came out, it reached number two on the *Billboard* 200 album chart. It sold over two million copies. After the huge success of *Tha Carter II*, nobody talked about Cash Money going out of business.

Lil Wayne had his first huge hit with "Go DJ."

21

In *Tha Carter II* Lil Wayne rapped about the music industry's bias against Southern rappers. For many in hip-hop, only the music from the East Coast was good. Others felt the same way about West Coast rappers. So artists like Lil Wayne were treated like they had no place in the business. Lil Wayne said he was tired of being patient for Southern rappers to get respect. When he was in New York City, he said, "People come up here—up North, East Coast—and they won't be half as good as us, but they'll be highly boasted," he says. "Put 'em next to me, I'll eat their head off."

In the same year Cash Money and Universal formed a new record label. They called it Young Money Entertainment. They made Lil Wayne president of the new label. This gave him the opportunity to release records under his own label. He could also sign artists to record on Young Money as well.

Lil Wayne surrounded himself with rappers he called the Young Money posse. These rappers included Jae Millz,

Gudda Gudda, Lloyd, Mack Maine, and Tyga. Even Birdman rapped for Lil Wayne. They worked on mixtapes that showed off the Young Money style. These mixtapes included a young female rapper named Nicki Minaj. Lil Wayne was so impressed with her style that he signed her to the label. A few years later Young Money signed the Canadian rapper Drake too.

Eventually Lil Wayne decided that he was more interested in recording than running a company. He gave control of Young Money Entertainment to high-school friend Cortez Bryant. Cortez would run Young Money and then work as a manager. He managed the careers of Lil Wayne, Drake, and Lil Twist.

Lil Wayne signed artists like Nicki Minaj and Mack Maine to Young Money Entertainment.

Hurricane Katrina

On August 29, 2005, Hurricane Katrina struck New Orleans. A hurricane can be disastrous anywhere. But New Orleans is unique compared to most cities. Much of the city is below sea level. The only things that kept New Orleans dry were walls and *levees* around the city. The hurricane brought in far more water than the levees and walls could hold. As the storm passed, about eighty percent of the city was underwater.

At first Lil Wayne did not think much about the storm. He was not in New Orleans when it hit. His home was damaged, but he could afford to replace it. His family was with him, so they were safe. But then he heard stories from home. Friends had drowned. People he knew could not get to shelters. Over 1,500 in Louisiana were killed by the effects of the hurricane. Some drowned. Others were hurt or sick and could not get help.

Many people felt that the government did not move quickly enough to help. On one of his mixtapes, Lil Wayne recorded a song called "Georgia … Bush." He criticized President Bush. He talked about people dying in "the pool." He complained that the police were too quick to shoot people. Some were simply stealing food in order to feed their families.

Lil Wayne traveled back to New Orleans. He handed out money for people to buy food and clothes. He also paid to rebuild a park. It was the same park he had played in as a child. But he moved his family and his business. First they went to Houston. Then they relocated to Miami.

Lil Wayne was deeply affected by Hurricane Katrina.

Lil Wayne continued to make mixtapes. He also recorded songs and uploaded them to the Internet. He would post them to his website. Fans could download them for free. Wayne also rapped on other artists' songs. He could get $150,000 to appear on just one song. He appeared on over seventy-five songs in just one year. Most artists are careful not to put too much music out. They worry that listeners will get tired of them. Lil Wayne clearly did not think the same way.

But Wayne was not the only person putting his music out. He was recording *Tha Carter III* in 2007. Someone who worked with him gave five of Wayne's songs to bootleggers. Soon the five songs were on the Internet. Universal was furious. People downloading the songs for free meant they did not make money on the songs. They had the music pulled from the web. Lil Wayne took a different approach. He took the five songs and made them into an EP. He released it, calling it *The Leak*. The EP said on the label, "Lil Wayne Approved." So all of the fans that heard about the leaked songs now had a way to buy them.

Universal was very unhappy with Wayne. They had to replace the songs that were supposed to be on *Tha Carter III*. They also felt they lost money on the free downloads and mixtapes. Lil Wayne did not care. He told them to wait until *Tha Carter III* was released. He was sure it would be a hit. Wayne told his friend and manager Cortez, "My work ethic is going to sell me. Nobody ain't doing what I've done. People will have to recognize that."

Lil Wayne gave his fans free downloads of his music.

Mainstream Success

Tha Carter III was supposed to come out in 2007. But because of the leaked tracks, it was delayed. Finally the album was released in May 2008. It sold over one million copies in its first week alone. Wayne had other hit artists on the album, including Jay-Z, Robin Thicke, Babyface, T-Pain, and Busta Rhymes.

Lil Wayne finally earned mainstream success. He was invited to appear on *Jimmy Kimmel Live*. He was invited to perform his hit singles "Lollipop" and "Got Money" on *Saturday Night Live*. Both shows helped him sell even more albums. *Tha Carter III* eventually sold more than three and a half million copies. He proved that Universal had no reason to worry about losing money on him.

That year was the highest point in Lil Wayne's career so far. "Lollipop" was the number-one song on the *Billboard* Hot 100 for five weeks. Three other singles from the album made it into the top twenty of the chart too. Lil Wayne received seven nominations for Grammy Awards. He won three of the awards, including Best Rap Album.

Wayne was also invited to perform at the Grammy Awards. He and Robin Thicke performed "Tie My Hands." The song referred to Hurricane Katrina. It described how helpless it made Wayne feel.

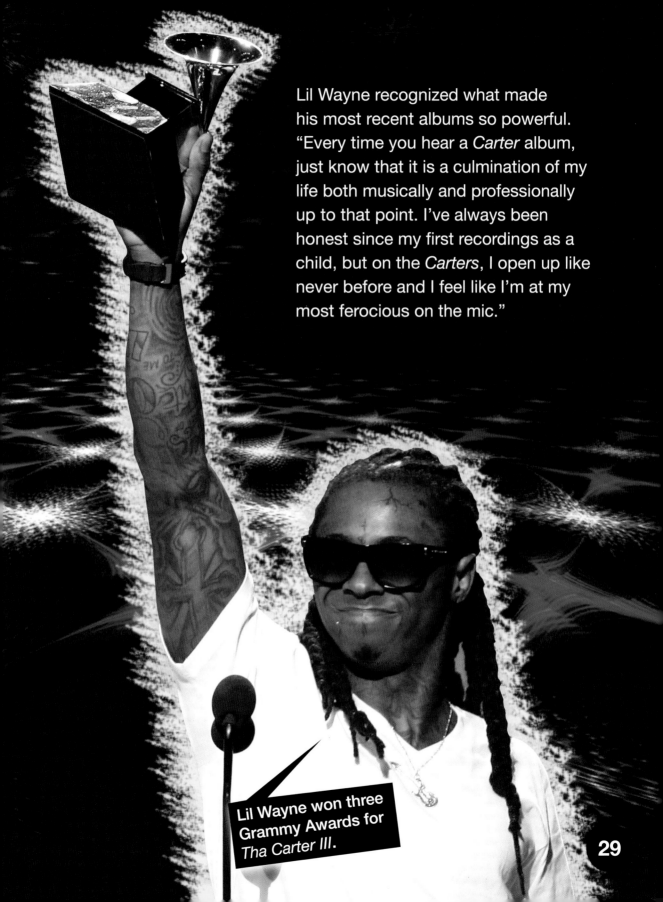

Lil Wayne recognized what made his most recent albums so powerful. "Every time you hear a *Carter* album, just know that it is a culmination of my life both musically and professionally up to that point. I've always been honest since my first recordings as a child, but on the *Carters*, I open up like never before and I feel like I'm at my most ferocious on the mic."

Lil Wayne won three Grammy Awards for *Tha Carter III*.

Lil Wayne was arrested in 2009 on drugs and weapons charges.

Lil Wayne has had his share of troubles. He has never made a secret of his love of marijuana. He was first arrested in 2006 in Atlanta, Georgia. He had marijuana and other drugs in his hotel room.

The next year he was in New York City. After a show Lil Wayne was standing near his tour bus smoking marijuana. Police officers saw him and placed him under arrest. The police then went onto the bus. They found more marijuana, as well as a gun.

While he waited for his trial, Lil Wayne went on tour. He also kept recording. In the summer of 2009, he performed with Drake, Young Jeezy, and Soulja Boy. He called it the *America's Most Wanted* tour.

Lil Wayne was finally sentenced to jail. He was placed in protective custody. This meant he was not around most of the other prisoners. Wayne and his lawyer worried that he would be a target of the other inmates. He spent most of his time in a cell that was only ten feet long by six feet wide. He had a bed, a desk, a sink, and a toilet in the space. He could spend eight hours a day in a room with a few other inmates. They could watch television or play cards.

Wayne worried about staying in fans' minds while he was in jail. Cortez helped solve the problem. He set up a website called "Weezy Thanx You." Wayne wrote letters and Cortez posted them to the site.

Wayne described how he spent his time. He explained that he worked out and read the Bible every day. Wayne also answered letters that fans sent him. He tried to encourage people who had their own problems. He talked about how much his website meant to him. "I laughed with some of you, reasoned with some of you, and even cried with some of you," he wrote. "I never imagined how much impact my words and life can have."

Life in jail was hard for Lil Wayne. He used to decide for himself what he would do every day. Jail was completely different. He had no control. At some point, someone gave Wayne an MP3 player, headphones, and a charger. None of these were allowed in jail. Wayne was sent to *solitary confinement* for breaking the rules. So instead of eight hours a day out of his cell, he only got one.

Wayne could not work in his recording studio while he was behind bars. But he did have recordings that were already on tape. He hired producers to put the songs together. His album *I Am Not a Human Being* was released while he was still in jail. Wayne was allowed to make occasional phone calls. So he rapped over the phone. Drake and Jay-Z used a recording of the call on the song "Light Up."

Lil Wayne was released on November 4, 2010. He had spent eight months in jail. Wayne was happy to be free. He saw friends and family. He was asked how he felt about being in jail. He said, "I was never scared, worried nor bothered by the situation."

Lil Wayne started performing again when he was released from prison.

Life After Jail

Rumor was that Lil Wayne had an album that would come out the day he got out of jail. This was only partly true. Wayne did have the album recorded before he went to jail. But as he served his sentence, he changed his mind. The songs were not what he wanted to say. He said, "I had a version of the album that I recorded before I went to jail last year. Then when I came home, I decided to start over for the most part. I had so many new ideas, some new outlooks on things. I wanted to give the people my most up-to-date perceptions of the world."

Some fans were not happy about the delay. They were waiting for new music. So Wayne put out a mixtape. He called it *Sorry 4 the Wait*. It came out in July 2011. Fans could download the mixtape songs for free while they waited for the album.

Finally in August 2011 Lil Wayne released *Tha Carter IV*. Like his last album, this album featured some of the hottest names in music: Rick Ross, Busta Rhymes, Drake, Jadakiss, Andre 3000, John Legend, and Bruno Mars. Just like *Tha Carter III*, this album was number one on the *Billboard* 200 the week it came out. It sold over two million copies. Wayne was very proud of the album. He said, "I wanted to make sure the LP went out with as much intensity as it begins with, so I assembled some of the best spitters in all of world to beat the track up."

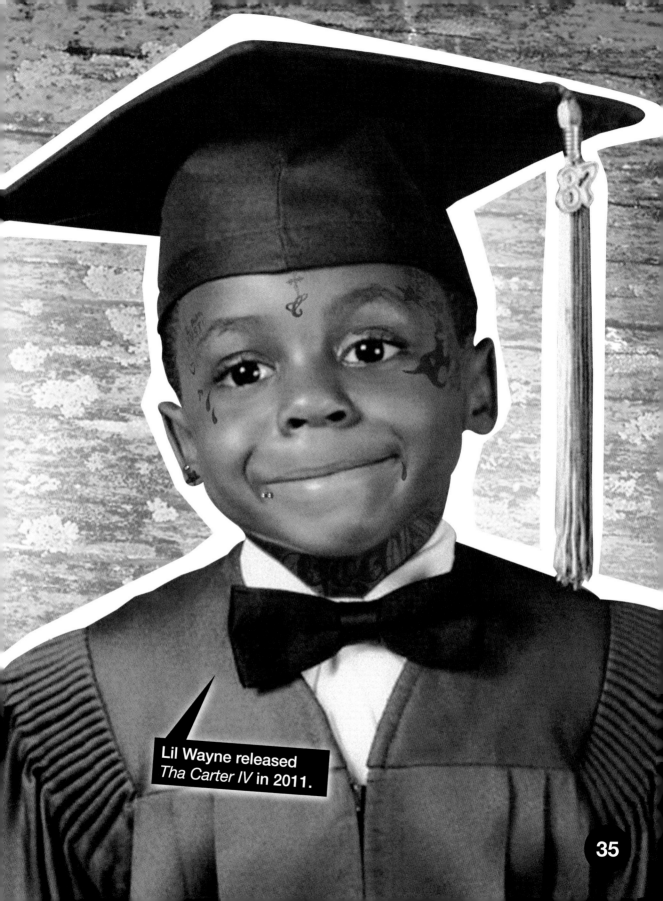

Lil Wayne released *Tha Carter IV* in 2011.

Through Lil Wayne's success and his troubles, he never forgot his roots. He has helped people all over the New Orleans area.

He started the One Family Foundation to help New Orleans youth. The foundation rebuilt the park and sports fields of his former school. The park was destroyed by Hurricane Katrina. He donated $200,000 to the city of New Orleans to rebuild the community center near his childhood home. Wayne hopes that by giving the kids a safe place to hang out, they will be safe. He also wants the kids to discover their talents. Wayne understands how important it is to become successful rather than trapped by poverty or crime.

Lil Wayne also combines his love of sports with helping others. He challenged people to bet on the college basketball finals. The money went toward the One Family Foundation. He also bowled with singer Nelly and athletes Chris Paul and Reggie Bush to raise more money for the people of New Orleans.

One of Lil Wayne's newer passions was skateboarding. He became interested in it after he was released from jail. He had a ramp built on the roof of his house and taught himself how to ride. As anyone learning how to skate, he fell a lot. At one point he needed nine stitches on his head. But this did not stop him. When Wayne performs, he books a skate park so he and his friends can skateboard afterward. Now Wayne is working with the makers of Mountain Dew to build a skate park in New Orleans. Wayne thinks that activities like sports will give kids choices that will keep them away from trouble.

Lil Wayne donated money and time to help rebuild New Orleans.

Lil Wayne is father to Reginae and three other children.

Lil Wayne met Antonia "Toya" Johnson when they were both kids in school. She became pregnant at fourteen. Their daughter, Reginae, was born when Toya and Wayne were both teenagers. Six years later Wayne married Toya. They loved each other, but Toya had a hard time dealing with him being away so much. Their marriage lasted only two years. Wayne stayed involved in Reginae's life. He and Toya remained good friends. Toya went on to become a reality television star on two different shows.

A few years after his divorce, Wayne had another child. Sarah Vivian gave birth to Dwayne Carter III in October 2008. He had another son less than a year after Dwayne was born. Actress Lauren London appeared in music videos, television shows, and movies. She is the mother of Cameron Carter. Just two months later, singer Nivea gave birth to Wayne's fourth child. His name is Neal Carter.

Lil Wayne is not romantically involved with any of the mothers of his children. But he does see his kids and supports them. Wayne understands what it is like to grow up without a father. He has said in interviews that he wants to be a real father for his kids. Reginae is a teen who wants to become a singer. So he plans on working with her to get her career off the ground.

Influences

Lil Wayne has very strong relationships with his Young Money artists. He gave them opportunities to become famous. For example, he had Nicki Minaj rapping on a number of his songs when she first started out. When she missed recording sessions, Lil Wayne fired her. But he gave her a second chance. After Nicki proved that she was willing to work as hard as he did, he hired her back. Now she is one of the top female rappers in the business.

Drake and Lil Wayne are close too. Wayne heard Drake's mixtape and invited him to come on tour with him. They spent a week together, recording and performing. From that moment on, Drake was a solid member of the Young Money crew.

The people in Wayne's life have supported him. But other artists have influenced his music. He says that one of his favorite musicians is the Artist Formerly Known as Prince. Many of Lil Wayne's songs use phrases from Prince's songs.

Wayne had other musical influences. Kurt Cobain was the lead singer of the *grunge* band Nirvana. Cobain's songs were meaningful to many youth growing up in the 1980s. He battled drug addiction and died when Wayne was just twelve years old. Wayne also greatly admired Jay-Z, one of the most successful rappers in the industry. Jay-Z sells millions of records and owns many entertainment companies.

As much as Wayne admired Jay-Z, they had a feud too. In a magazine interview, Wayne said about Jay-Z, "It's not your house anymore and I'm better than you." Jay-Z criticized Wayne for his drug use in a diss song with fellow rapper T.I. Lil Wayne's response was to make fun of how old Jay-Z was.

Lil Wayne performed with one of his heroes, Jay-Z.

Football player JaMarcus Russell lost a promising career because of his use of "syrup."

Lil Wayne was arrested more than once for having marijuana. He has said more than once that marijuana should not be against the law. In an interview Wayne said, "I will stand up for marijuana any day ... I'm a rapper. That's who I am … and I am a gangster and I do what I want. And I love to smoke. And I smoke." After his arrests in Georgia and New York, Wayne was arrested two more times. He was caught with marijuana and other drugs on his tour bus in Arizona and Texas. Wayne was placed on three years' probation in Arizona for his crime. In order to stay out of jail, Wayne agreed to stop using marijuana.

Wayne also used another drug for a long time—"purple drank." This purple liquid is cough medicine with a painkiller added to it. People can get the medicine from a doctor for severe coughs and colds. But many people use the medicine to get high.

Wayne called it his "syrup." He often mixed it with sweet sodas. Then he would pour it into a cup that he kept with him all day. When the syrup in his cup ran out, he would just pour more. Purple drank is very dangerous. Some people have died from it. But it is very popular with hip-hop artists and athletes.

Even though he liked feeling high, the syrup was hard on Wayne. He said, "It messes up your stomach; your stomach hurt real, real bad. It's an excruciating pain." So in May 2009 he stopped using it. His fans may not have known he stopped because he continued to rap about syrup.

One of Lil Wayne's biggest passions is sports. He has appeared on ESPN and writes for their magazine. He loves tennis, football, hockey, basketball, and baseball. Wayne is even a great bowler. He enjoys the sport so much that he has had custom bowling balls made.

Wayne has also found his way into television and movies. He has appeared in the movie *Freaknik: The Musical*. He has appeared in a number of television shows and movies, like *The Boondocks* and *The Roaches*. He has even used his voice for animated shows, like the movie *The Good Dinosaur*.

Trukfit is Lil Wayne's line of clothes. He put his name on a line of T-shirts, hooded sweatshirts, and baseball caps. His clothes are sold in department stores around the United States.

Wayne has also returned to school. Because he dropped out of high school, he earned his GED. Then Wayne signed up for college classes. He started by taking classes at the University of Houston. But he found that he traveled too much to attend classes in a classroom. So Wayne changed to the University of Phoenix. They offer classes over the Internet. Wayne can now attend classes no matter where he is. He is studying psychology.

What may surprise fans most are Wayne's plans to retire. He figures he will stop recording by the time he is thirty-five years old. He wants time to spend with his children. He wants to focus on the careers of his Young Money artists. Will he miss it? Wayne answered, "I feel like I'll be a new me, and how good is that? To actually be opening a brand-new door of life at thirty-five? That'd be awesome. Totally awesome. I'm looking forward to it."

Lil Wayne and Kenny Mayne appeared on ESPN together.

Vocabulary

bias	(noun)	prejudice
Billboard	(noun)	magazine that covers the music industry, including record and album sales
bootlegger	(noun)	a person who sells illegal copies of something, like clothes or music
contract	(noun)	an agreement between two people, between two companies, or between a person and a company
critic	(noun)	a person who judges
diss	(adjective)	insulting
DJ	(noun)	a person who plays records or mixes records, usually at a party or club
EP	(noun)	an extended play recording, usually longer than a single but shorter than an album
feud	(noun)	a fight that lasts over a long time
GED	(noun)	General Equivalency Degree, an alternative to a high-school diploma
Grammy Award	(noun)	an award given to the best recording artists every year by The Recording Academy
grunge	(adjective)	a style of music with a strong guitar and loose vocals
hip-hop	(adjective or noun)	using strong beats and chanted words; music that uses strong beats and chanted words
levee	(noun)	built-up land to prevent flooding

mainstream	(adjective)	popular with most people
manager	(noun)	a person who does business on someone's behalf, a representative
marijuana	(noun)	dried leaves of a plant that are smoked as a drug
minor	(noun)	a person under the age of eighteen
mixtape	(noun)	a CD of songs made without a record company
pop	(adjective or noun)	generally appealing; a watered-down version of rock and roll
probation	(noun)	a period of time that criminals are supervised after they have served their sentence
producer	(noun)	a person who raises money to create a song, a stage show, and so on
profanity	(noun)	swearing or other inappropriate language
promote	(verb)	to sell or advertise for a product
R&B	(noun)	rhythm-and-blues, a type of music with repetitious rhythms and simple melodies
rap	(adjective, verb, or noun)	spoken with rhythm; to speak with rhythm; music in which words are spoken in rhythm
reputation	(noun)	the way a person or persons are judged
single	(noun)	one song, usually from an album
solitary confinement	(noun)	a jail cell where the prisoner has little to no contact with other people
swagger	(noun)	pride or obvious confidence
trademark	(adjective)	a way a person or thing is identified

Photo Credits

AP Images: Amanda Edwards/PictureGroup p. 11; Anja Niedringhaus/Associated Press pp. 12–13; Kevork Djansezian/Associated Press pp. 14–15; Tony Gutierrez/Associated Press pp. 18–19; Ben Rose/PictureGroup pp. 22–23; Louis Lanzano/Associated Press p. 30; Associated Press p. 35

Getty Images: Mark Davis/Getty Images Entertainment pp. 4–5; Imeh Akpanudosen/Getty Images Entertainment pp. 6–7; John Wang/Photographer's Choice RF pp. 8–9; Shawn Thew/Getty Images News pp. 16–17; L. Cohen/WireImage pp. 20–21; Michael Lewis/National Geographic pp. 24–25; Theo Wargo/WireImage p. 27; John Shearer/WireImage p. 29; Scott Legato/FilmMagic p. 33; John Parra/WireImage p. 37; Johnny Nunez/WireImage pp. 38–39; Jeff Gross/Getty Images Sport pp. 42–43; Alexander Tamargo/Getty Images Entertainment pp. 44–45

Rex Features: PictureGroup Cover; Sipa Press/Rex Features pp. 40–41